Humvees
and Other Military Vehicles

Jay H. Smith

Reading consultant:

John Manning, Professor of Reading

University of Minnesota

Capstone Press

MINNEAPOLIS

Capstone Press • 2440 Fernbrook Lane • Minneapolis, MN 55447

Editorial Director   John Coughlan
Managing Editor   John Martin
Copy Editor   Gil Chandler

Library of Congress Cataloging-in-Publication Data

Smith, Jay H.
   Humvees and other military vehicles / by Jay H. Smith.
      p. cm.-- (Wheels)
   Includes bibliographical references and index.
   ISBN 1-56065-219-5
   1. High Mobility Multipurpose Wheeled Vehicle--Juvenile
   literature. 2. Land-Rover truck--Juvenile literature. 3.
   Desert patrol vehicle--Juvenile literature. [1. Vehicles,
   Military.]   I. Title. II. Series: Wheels (Minneapolis, Minn.)
UG618.S63   1995
623.7'47--dc20   94-22825
                                                      CIP
                                                      AC

Table of Contents

Chapter 1
The Humvee

You're a soldier in the **Gulf War** (1991). Your unit is told to cross 100 miles (160 kilometers) of desert. The land is hot, dry, and rough enough to make a camel cry. Do you complain? No! You jump into your Humvee and take off.

Your seven-foot (about two-meter) wide vehicle slides straight down a wall of sand. The roaring diesel engine drowns out your shouts. At the base of the wall, the bombed-out frames of enemy jeeps lie on the desert floor. The Humvee rolls over them as if they were tin cans.

You come to a wide river, but you don't slow down. Your monster vehicle pushes straight through four feet (1.25 meters) of water. Inside, water and mud rise up to your waist.

On the other side of the river, there's a hill of sand and rock 30 feet (about nine meters) high. Your vehicle picks its way up the wall, wheel by wheel. There seems to be no way it could go straight up like this. You're sure it will fall over. But it doesn't. Not a Humvee. In a few minutes you are on top of the hill.

Thousands of miles away, a movie star is watching television coverage of **Operation Desert Storm**. The camera has followed your Humvee's charge up the wall. Arnold Schwarzenegger is thinking: "I love that ugly machine! I have to have one."

Humvee and Hummer

Arnold got what he wanted–the first **civilian** model of the Humvee. The army calls its version of this rugged vehicle the Humvee (short for High **Mobility** Multipurpose

Humvees prepare for action during Operation Desert Storm.

Wheeled Vehicle). Arnold and other non-military buyers drive the civilian version, called the Hummer. Soldiers and civilians drive basically the same machine, but only the military can mount guns on theirs.

Where the Humvee Came From

In 1980 the United States Army started thinking about replacing its fleet of **transport** carriers. There were problems with the carriers it was using at the time.

The jeep, in use since 1940, was too slow and often tipped over on sharp turns. The Gama Goat was a useful **amphibious** vehicle. It could cover any kind of **terrain**. But it was too small and too loud. The Dodge three-quarter-ton pickup and the Chevrolet Blazer were faster, but they were not very good off-road vehicles.

Army leaders were looking for a good, tough, vehicle that could meet all their needs. So they selected three companies to build **prototypes**. One of these companies was AM General of Mishawaka, Indiana.

AM General's prototype, the Humvees, was the clear winner among the three. It passed

The jeep served the Army as an all-purpose transport vehicle.

every test. The company won a contract to produce more of the new Humvees. In 1985, the Humvee joined the army. In 1994, there were more than 100,000 in the United States military fleet.

Heavyweight Champion

What makes the Humvee so tough? It sits 16 inches (40.5 centimeters) above the ground. This allows it to climb over almost anything.

Its standard V-8 engine has 150 **horsepower** and 250 pounds (95 kilograms) of **maximum torque**. It can haul about 10,000 pounds (4,536 kilograms) and carry 4,000 pounds (1,814 kilograms).

Its huge tires are set far apart for **stability**. There is even a switch on the dashboard to inflate or deflate the tires, depending on terrain conditions. The Humvee has four-wheel **independent suspension** and full-time,

The Humvee can handle terrain that would stop most vehicles dead in their tracks.

independent **four-wheel drive**. This makes it the only true four-wheel-drive vehicle.

The Humvee weighs more than 6,000 pounds (2,722 kilograms). Its **chassis** is 6 feet (1.8 meters) high, 15 feet (4.5 meters) long, and 7 feet (2.1 meters) wide. Its body is made of aircraft aluminum over a steel frame. It is fastened together with 2,800 **rivets**.

The Humvee comes with handles on its chassis. With a heavy chain attached to those handles, a helicopter can lift a Humvee to a remote site where it is needed. The handles also serve as parachute ties. Transport planes dropped Humvees by parachute in Operation Desert Storm. The Humvees always landed on their tires.

It pays to be tough. During the Gulf War, one Humvee hit a land mine. The explosion caused some damage, but not enough to stop the vehicle from going another 30 miles (48 kilometers) to safety. No one was seriously hurt.

Chapter 2

The Hummer

There are many different types of Humvees and Hummers. For the army, AM General makes a cargo troop carrier, a tow-missile, an **armament** carrier, a maxi-ambulance, and a heavy truck.

For civilians, the Hummer comes as a utility truck, a snowplow, a scooploader, a salt-spreader, or a fire truck. You can buy a two- or four-passenger hardtop, a canvas-top, or a four-

With a machine gun mounted on its roof, the Humvee becomes a mobile weapon that can travel anywhere.

passenger wagon. You can even buy Hummers with camouflage paint.

Some people equip their vehicles in unusual ways. Arnold Schwarzenegger put a big stereo and a telephone in his Hummer. He also had "Terminator" painted on the sides.

Racing Hummers

In 1993 a tough off-road race called the Baja 1000 was held in Baja California. This thin desert peninsula stretches south from the United States-Mexico border. The race attracts fans who want to see the latest in 4x4 technology. It is a race of speed, but endurance is even more important.

Jeeps, Ford F150s, Land Rovers, and Range Rovers entered the race. Two Hummers also competed. The spectators laughed, because they thought Hummers were just too big to race. Top speed in a Hummer is 80 miles (128 kilometers) per hour, and that is on hard, flat surfaces.

The Hummers just kept plugging along over the course's difficult terrain. Many other vehicles broke down or fell behind, and the Hummers came in first and second.

Hummers are tough enough to maintain high speed over rocks and sand.

Chapter 3

The Land Rover

In third place in the 1993 Baja 1000 was a Land Rover. The Land Rover is a living 4x4 legend. It was created in England by the brothers Maurice and Spencer Wilks in 1947. They made the first Rover from the parts of army surplus jeeps.

The Wilks brothers designed their new four-wheel-drive for farm use. Soon the demand for the Rover was more than they could handle. Everyone wanted one of these sturdy vehicles.

In 1948 the British Army accepted two vehicles from the Rover Company for testing. These four-wheelers were driven day and night over rugged terrain. They splashed through ponds and bounced up and down steep slopes. They raced against other military vehicles— and won. The army asked for more Land Rovers right away.

Every year brought improvements in the Land Rover. Different versions were built for every kind of use. The British Army adopted the Land Rover as its standard 4x4 in 1956. Soon after that, the Land Rover was known as the world's most **versatile** vehicle.

The Rover turned out to be the most useful vehicle in the **Korean War** (1950-1953). Besides carrying troops and hauling trailers and weapons, it was used as an ambulance. Rovers made handy mobile missile launchers as well. One long-range desert Land Rover was painted a dull pink to blend into the desert haze. It became known as the "Pink Panther."

The Range of the Rover

The Land Rover continues to be a popular 4x4. Military and police forces all over the world use it. The British still love their

Rovers, which are now made by the British Leyland Company. There are Rover clubs and Rover fans all over Britain.

In 1994 Land Rover brought out a new model, the Defender 90. Small and loud, it quickly won the title "4x4 of the Year."

The Range Rover, a British four-wheel-drive, tackles rough terrain with ease.

Chapter 4

The Desert Patrol Vehicle

The big Humvee was the star of the war in the Persian Gulf. Another vehicle was also very important to this successful campaign. This vehicle was small, light, and fast. It was especially good at escaping enemy radar. It was a dune buggy called the Desert Patrol Vehicle, or DPV.

Behind the scenes, the United States Navy SEALs (Sea, Air, and Land teams) raced DPVs across enemy lines. Their special mission was to rescue downed pilots and to gather information.

From Dunes to Desert

The modified dune buggy "goes wherever a motorcycle can go and a Hummer can't," says Michael Thomas. Thomas is the president of Chenoweth Racing, the small company in El Cajon, California, that makes these special vehicles. Chenoweth has been making dune buggies with a lightweight **tubular** chassis since the 1970s.

The DPV is small enough to slip through enemy radar, but large enough to carry guns, a three person crew, and extra cargo.

The United States Navy became interested in the vehicles in 1977. At first the Navy used them as targets during training exercises. Naval officers realized that if the buggies could race all over the California desert, they could travel in other deserts, too.

The Desert Patrol Vehicle at Work

The DPV is an effective weapon in wartime. Its tubular frame makes it hard for an enemy to detect on radar.

The speed of the DPV is important, too. It can go from zero to 30 miles (48 kilometers) per hour in four seconds. Top speed is close to 100 miles (160 kilometers) per hour.

The Desert Patrol Vehicle can run on flat tires over razor-sharp rocks. It can also make sharp turns without tipping over. A harness straps in the three passengers so they won't bounce out.

The DPV has many extra features. There are baskets on the sides of the frame for carrying food, water, ammunition, or wounded soldiers. The buggy has racks for anti-tank missiles and shoulder-launched missiles. A machine gun or grenade launcher fits into top and rear mounts. Armed with these weapons, the DPV becomes dangerous.

Chapter 5

Tanks

The tank is the **ultimate** armored vehicle. It is at the center of every defense system. When the tank first took part in battle, however, it looked like a failure.

The British invented the tank during **World War I** (1914-1918). It was supposed to protect soldiers against the new heavy machine guns of the German army. Riding in the armored vehicle was a safe way to get across rough terrain under heavy fire.

Early tanks did not move fast or smoothly. They often tipped over. And their slowness made them easy targets for the enemy. The British almost gave up on them.

After the war, designers and builders made improvements in the tank. In **World War II** (1939-1945) army **tactics** had changed completely. The tanks had become effective fighting vehicles.

The tanks moved smoothly through weak points in the enemy lines. They crushed everything in their path. Cannons on top of the tanks could fire in all directions. Their accurate guns could destroy troops, supplies, fortifications, and enemy tanks.

Anti-Tank Weapons and Armor

There are several weapons used against the modern tank.

• With HEAT (High Explosive Anti-Tank) rounds, a stream of red hot metal pierces the tank's armor and burns the crew inside to death.

Tanks and other armored vehicles make up the core of the modern ground force.

• HESH (High Explosive Squash Head) rounds crumble when they hit the tank. The shock waves from the impact and explosion destroy the tank and kill the crew.

• APDS (Armor Piercing Discarding Sabot) rounds have **tungsten carbide** or **uranium** cores and a **sabot** that falls off as it leaves the

Modern tanks carry a variety of weapons as well as complicated radar systems.

gun barrel. This pierces the tank's armor and causes it to break apart.

Chobham Armor

Armor designers try to keep up with the latest anti-tank systems. The British have developed **Chobham armor**. Its metal composition is top secret. It has been a successful armor against some of the most powerful anti-tank weapons.

Reactive armor is made of pieces that explode when hit by an anti-tank round. This causes the round to lose its force.

The newest kind of armor is called **active-reactive armor**. An explosive charge in the surface of active-reactive armor stops the anti-tank round.

Today there are hundreds of kinds of tanks. Each has its special use.

The M1

The best-known of American tanks is the M1 Abrams Main Battle Tank. It carries four men and two machine guns. The main gun finds its target with a computer. The M1 is constantly being improved, although it is already the most advanced tank in the world.

The M551 Sheridan Light Tank

The M551 Sheridan Light Tank has been with the United States Army since 1966. It served in the Gulf War with Humvees and Desert Patrol Vehicles.

Left and *above*, the M1 Abrams Main Battle Tank

The Sheridan's chief feature is its missile launcher. When a missile leaves the launcher, four fins and a tail unfold. A two-way **infrared** command link guides the missile to its target.

The Bradley

The Bradley Fighting Vehicle System is the army's newest armored vehicle. It weighs

about 50,000 pounds (22,700 kilograms) and can carry a full squad of infantry soldiers.

The Bradley has day and night **thermal vision**, equipment that "sees" by detecting heat sources. With this feature, the Bradley can operate at any time. There's no need for daylight to aim its weapons.

Space-**laminate** armor protects the Bradley. Made of lightweight aluminum, it is faster than a steel tank, but can be destroyed easily by an anti-tank missile.

Armored vehicles are in the army to stay. They may become bigger. They may carry and protect more troops. Or new technology and new weapons systems may make them smaller. They are sure to become more deadly.

A tank crew has to master the use of a wide variety of complex electronic equipment.

Glossary

active-reactive armor–armor with an explosive charge in its surface

amphibious–able to operate on land and water

armament–attacking weapons, including guns and bombs

chassis–the framework that lies under a motor vehicle

Chobham armor–a top-secret armor developed by the British

civilian–a person not in military service

four-wheel drive–a vehicle with all four wheels linked to the engine

Gulf War–a conflict between the United States and its allies against Iraq in the Persian Gulf region in 1991

horsepower–a unit used to measure the power of an engine

independent suspension–the ability of a vehicle's wheel to move independently of the others

infrared–invisible light rays that can be detected by special equipment. Infrared sensors allow soldiers to detect objects or enemy at night.

Korean War–a war from 1950 to 1953, in which the United States and South Korea fought North Korea

laminate–a cover made up of thin layers of metal

maximum torque–highest number of rotations

mobility–ability to move

Operation Desert Storm–the name for the ground battle that took place during the Gulf War in 1991. The United States and its allies fought against Iraq, after Iraq invaded Kuwait.

prototype–the first model made of a vehicle

reactive armor–armor that explodes when hit by an anti-tank round

rivets–metal fasteners

sabot–a soft metal clip attached to a missile to keep it in place

stability–the state of being stable or firm

tactics–the science of using military forces

terrain–the natural features of the land

thermal vision–the ability to see in the dark with machinery that detects heat sources

transport–the act of carrying from one place to another, especially over long distances

tubular–made out of tubes

tungsten carbide–a hard, heat-resistant metal containing carbon

ultimate–the very latest or best

uranium–a hard, heavy radioactive material

versatile–able to do many different things

World War I–a war in Europe from 1914 to 1918 in which the United States, the British, and their allies fought against Germany

World War II–a war in Europe, Asia, the Pacific, and Africa from 1939 to 1945, in which the United States fought with its allies against Germany, Japan, and Italy.

To Learn More

Green, Michael. *Hummer.* Osceola, WI: Motorbooks International, 1992.

Miller, David. *New Illustrated Guide to Modern Tanks and Fighting Vehicles.* New York: Smithmark Publishers, 1992.

Taylor, James. *The Land Rover.* Croydon, England: Motor Racing Publications Ltd., 1988.

Norman, C.J. *Tanks.* New York: Franklin Watts, 1986.

Stephen, R.J. *The Picture World of Tanks.* New York: Franklin Watts, 1990.

Hogg, Ian V. *Tanks and Armored Vehicles.* New York: Franklin Watts, 1984.

You can read articles about Humvees and other military vehicles in these magazines: *Military Vehicles, Military Hobbies,* and *Land Rover Owner International.*

Some Useful Addresses

Land Rover Owners Association
P.O. Box 6836
Oakland, CA 94603

U.S. Army Center of Military History
1099 14th Street N.W.
Washington, D.C. 20005-3402

Patton Museum of Cavalry and Armor
4554 Fayette Avenue
Fort Knox, KY 40121-0208

UDT/SEAL Museum
3300 North A1A
Hutchinson Island
Fort Pierce, FL 34949

The War Memorial Museum of Virginia
8285 Warwick Boulevard
Huntington Park
Newport News, VA 23607

Index

Photo Credits: